Candy

"Tried and True military cadences <u>YOU</u> never heard"

*To one of the realist
Nco's on earth!!*

Brett Thomas

Brett Thomas

ISBN-13: 978-1541152885

ISBN-10: 1541152883

DEDICATION

Cadence Candy is dedicated to military members that search for the good in everything. We wrote these cadences to motivate, uplift and inspire all who choose to read, memorize and call them.

INTRODUCTION

Every cadence here has been tried and truly enjoyed by our military all around the world. This book stands out to the masses because the cadences are uplifting and positive affirmations. One line of cadence is sung by the cadence caller. Unless noted otherwise-that exact line is repeated by the formation. Motivational cadences bring out the best in everyone. Feel free to edit any questionable words or phrases to keep them politically correct. Imagination and rhythm play a major key in cadence calling. Cadence Candy is separated into two parts-Marching Cadence Candy and Running Cadence Candy. Every verse is counted as one line of cadence unless noted otherwise.

All military branches will enjoy perusing this vast collection of original military cadences...Cadence Candy.

CADENCE CANDY

MARCHING CADENCE CANDY

2000 NOW

It's the 2000 now cadence
Betcha by golly wow
Standing tall like Collin Powell
We make enemies, bow down
Betcha by golly wow
It's the 2000 now cadence
Betcha by golly will
Load and unload, trained to kill
We make enemies, just chill
Betcha by golly will
It's the 2000 now cadence
Betcha by golly Hooah!!
All eyes on me like Tupac Shakur
I ain't mad at cha, Hooah!!
I get around, and the getting is good
Betcha by golly Hooah!!

ARMY IS THE NAME

U.S. Army is the name
Signal is our thing
Respect the leadership all around
Building Signal from the ground

U.S. Army household name
It's in our hearts and through our veins
See the Soldier in our eyes
Shining brightly from inside

AS THE WORLD TURNS

As the world turns
And the fire burns
Forget that trash talk, it's none of my concern
I wheel and I deal
I hustle and I flow
I'm like a Tonka-Truck
I'm indestructible
I can't be stopped, nor hopped to be contained
I keep it copasetic and I'm flyer
Than a plane
I move like the wind
Travel through the trees
I'm invisible your best bet is to deceive
Try if you may
I'll still be on top
And the way I steal the show
You might want to call the cops
So dial 911 tell them how you feel
About me keeping fish hooked without
A rod or a reel
So see what you've been missing
Sooner then you should
I live a soldier's life

BELIEVE IT OR NOT

Believe it or not
I'm hotter than a lava rock
Clever as a fox
More secure then fort Knox
I put the marks on the paper
You connect the dots
I write the part
You play the part
I coming to your town soon
Pick – a spot
So we can get acquainted
I'll draw a Picture
And I'll let you paint it
And you can keep it
Only if you maintain it
I'm saying
That's cool aint it!
Believe it or not

BLUE

You can talk the talk 'til you're blue in the face
You gotta walk the walk you wanna win the race
You can run that yopper 'til your face turn blue
But action is what, gets you through
You can work your fingers 'til your hands turn blue
But using your mind, is working too
Look at the blue sky, the sky is the limit
Put passion into it, and you'll be winning

BRINGING PAIN

Been bringing pain, way before high school
Been bringing rain call me Mr. Typhoon
Your ace boon coon's, ace boon coon
Come with all the trimmings like a boom boom room
I do it and invent blue prints
Don't be clueless with no intent
I'm electric with cadence like a outlet
Shocking young soldiers like "Owe Shit!"
 Been bringing Pain!

CAME IN THE GAME

Came in the game with a rule book
I'm a super Soldier with a tool box
My son said "You a fool Pop"
I said "What you said Boi"
He said "Fool as in cool Pop"
So you know that I'm the truth huh?
They gave me staff after basic training
Now I'm working in staff, basically training
I'm a problem solver
Straight shooter like revolvers
Getting green like the Olive garden
Not Mary Jane I'm talking U.S. dollars

CLOCK WORK

I enjoy myself day in and day out
Relish every milli-second
Til my life fades out
I got a clock that escapes
With no wings on the run
I guess time flies
When you have fun
Seconds add up past
Minutes and hours
Hours turn to days
Days turn to dollars
Dollars make cents (sense)
So I buy the cement
To build a foundation
And annihilate hating

COMMISSARY

I went to the commissary
And I flash my I.D.
Then I went to isle one
And I got myself some cheese
Got myself some eggs
Some milk and some sardines
Then I got me a Cornish hen
Oh, yeah, I'm going to eat
I went and got some sausage
A bag of ice glazed chicken
Then I got me some T-bones
Then I got me some sugar
Then I went to isle three

I got me some noodles
I got me some ribeye's
And some New York strips
I got myself a slab of ribs
And some baby back tips
Then I went to the bakery
And got myself some croissants
I got me some anti-pasta
They had everything I wanted
Then I went to the checkout
Right by the ATM
I took out some cash
And then I paid the cashier
Then the bagger bagged me up
And brought my groceries to the car
So I gave him three dollars
He said "thank you very much"
I went to the commissary

GO THE EXTRA MILE

Go the extra mile
Do it with a smile
Do it with some style
Do it for your child
Keep, keep going
Keep, keep going
Move with a purpose
Are you rabbit or a tortoise?
Slow and steady wins the race
You just keep a steady pace
Go the extra mile …

HEAD, SHOULDERS, KNEES AND TOES

Head, shoulders, knees and toes
Above competition nearly anything goes
You have one mouth and two ears
Hush one time and double up on what you hear
Call me big dawg, cause my dynamic pedigree
Allow me to introduce you to the mega me
You'll get addicted to my style like
methamphetamines
But I'm, all about the better things
You know what I'm saying
Pigs get fat, hogs get slaughtered
Free birds sing caged birds don't bother
Head, shoulders, knees and toes

HERE BY POPULAR DEMAND

Here by popular demand I'm the man
This right here is the beginning of your ending
I got the game sewed up, mentally mended
Serge leave weak troops choked and offended
With presidential cadence like I wrote the
amendments
Monumental status like Abraham Lincoln
But y'all thinking it's all about the Franklins
Here's a penny for your thoughts
Soon it'll add up
I'm in your face to finish
Like "and what!!"
Here by popular demand I'm the man

I AIN'T A GAMBLING MAN

I ain't a gambling man
But I'll bet you a bill
I'm a soldier through and through
With a license to kill
Like Mike Tyson I'm I'll
With a Ice cold chill
Beat the bricks off an enemy
Let's make a deal
I'm ruthless with mass appeal
Hard to the core
Like I'm cast in steel
Cadence – magic
You can't cop – a – feel

IF YOU GO AGAINST ME

If you go against me …
Bring intense beef
I 'am the grill man!!
I got intense heat
I'll chop the beef up
Until its minced meat …

If you go against me…

I GOT A FRIEND

I got a friend in Arizona
We have fun all day and at night we turn-up
I got a friend in New York City
She's real tall and very pretty
I got a friend living in Croatia
She said she never met a hater
I got a friend in South Carolina
He's my barber and he does my line up
I got a friend came down from TX
Got 32 inch rims on a brand new Lexus
I got a friend that lives in Georgia
Favorite team is the George Town Hoyas

I JOINED THE ARMY

I joined the Army to get in shape
Now I'm lean and mean like a jungle ape
I joined the Army to get some schooling
When I get out I can do some cooling
Wake up in the morning throw on my uniform
Tie up my boots, grab my soldier tools
Left, right, left, right out the door
Work all day 'til my feet get sore

THE WINDOW

The window, the window
I'll throw you out the window
If you don't say a rhyme and say it on time
I'll throw you out the window
Simple Simon was a pie man
Now he's shining like a diamond
Cause he sold his pie shops
In every state on every block
On every door, he would knock
And if they answered he would talk
Real talk, talk,talk, talk
The window, the window
I'll throw you out the window
If you don't say a rhyme and say it on time
I'll throw you out the window
Peter Peter pumpkin eater
Had a wife and use to beat her
Until one day she stood her ground
Told him "it ain't going down"
Then he stumbled and he mumbled
He was drunk off Hennessey
He used to drink it heavily
He said "it felt heavenly"
But you ain't heard that from me
The window, the window
I'll throw you out the window
If you don't say a rhyme and say it on time
I'll throw you out the window
Little Miss Muffet
The pimps' puppet
Eating beans and rice
Along came her pimp

In a Cadillac and high priced ice
He said "grab your beans and rice
Come with me and you'll get meat
Your only half of what you can be"
Allow me to make you complete
The window, the window
I'll throw you out the window
If you don't say a rhyme and say it on time
I'll throw you out the window
Mary Mary little Locket
Kept a pistol in her pocket
When trouble came, she would cock it
And set fire to it like a rocket
I know to some this sounds insane
She also had a sniper's aim
Her bullets fly between your eyes
And pass right through your brain
The window, the window
I'll throw you out the window
If you don't say a rhyme and say it on time
I'll throw you out the window
Sally sold sea shells
Down by the sea shore
Until one day she saw Simon
And his pie stores
She left the shore quick, quick, quick
Sored in a plane and took a trip
To where they give out business loans
Now Sally has stores of her own
The window, the window
I'll throw you out the window
If you don't say a rhyme and say it on time
I'll throw you out the window

I MADE A CHANGE

I made a change for the better
I'm not talking suits and ties
The change for the better
Happened in my mind
I kilt the old me
Left procrastination behind
I get sensations in my spine
When I grind all the time
The enthusiasm
That I'm shooting at them
Have them whooping and hollering
I made a change for the better

I'M UP EARLY

I'm up early, early early ear-ly
I go to work, work work, work
I get dirty, dirty dirt dir-ty
I'm a leader, leader, leader, lea-der
Highly motivated
Highly dedicated
From start to finish
From beginning to end
I'm up early, early, early, ear-ly

LASTING IMPRESSIONS

We leave lasting impressions
Like permanent markers
We blast off in each session
Not concerned if we spark ya!
The price is right
We'll Bob Bark ya
Come on down
And get this punishment partner
Who want to challenge the soldiers?
Raise your hand
We cut to the chase
Like a razor can!
Just face it Fam!

LAST NIGHT

Last night and the night before
I met my baby at the candy store
She bought me ice cream
She bought me cake
She bought me home with a belly ache
Mama, Mama I am sick
She said call the Dr. quick, quick, quick
Dr., Dr. Will I die?
He said close your eyes and count to 5
1, 2, 3 4, 5
The next thing you know, I'm alive
See that house on top of that hill
That's where me and my baby live
Give me a piece a meat
Give me a piece a bread
Come on baby lets go to bed!!!

LET IT BE KNOWN

Let it be known
Let it be shown
In every song
King of the throne
Big on the beat
Elephantid us
Golden touch
King Midas
Super Star
When I perform
Above average
Surpass the norm
Man, I mean this
I'm a genius
More consistent
Than a machine is

LOCK AND LOAD (LET THE COLD WINDS BLOW)

Lock and load, lock and load
M -16 qualified
Bullets sing a Lullaby
Fye, fye fye, fye !! (gun shot noise)

Lock and load, lock and load
Let the marksmen go
Let the sharpshooters go next
Just know the experts are the best

Lock and load, lock and load
M – 4 qualified
Bullets sing a Lullaby
Fye, fye, fye, fye !!

LOOK UP

Look up in the sky
And see forever
The world is yours
I'm on another level
Like NASA
I burn up the gravel
Like a NASCAR
I fly through the sky
Like rumors of a king
I'll never die
I'm a legend in the game
Look up in the sky

NEVER SCARED

I'm never scared
You're more than scary
My style,
More than varies
Extraordinary
Leave the battle field
Like a mortuary
Crush competition
Keys in the ignition
Bulldoze who oppose
With hailstone flows
Mr. Reliable
Check the way I fire tools
And Inspire troops
Then keep a eye out
Eye out for the truth

OUTWARDLY AWKWARD

Outwardly awkward
Original misfit
Walk real quiet
Carry a big stick
Some say cockiness
Others say arrogance
I could careless
I know its confidence
Consider me to be
A spontaneous monument

PATIENCE IS A VIRTUE

Patience is a virtue
I thought you knew
You can act like you don't
But what's the point, what's the point
Hurry up and wait
Hurry up and wait
You volunteered for
Hurry up and wait

PLAN A

If plan A doesn't work
I'll do plan B
If plan B doesn't work
I'll do plan C
If plan C doesn't work
I'll do plan D
If plan D doesn't work
I'll do plan E
The moral to the story is
Plan ahead and keep ideas flowing
If plan E doesn't work
I'll do plan F
If plan F doesn't work
I'll do plan G..

PLANT A SEED

Dig a hole in the land
Plant a seed in the land
Plant a seed of success
Grow success from the seed
The seeds are ideas
Grow your ideas
Take action on your goals
Take action every day
Success will be yours
Your life will be fun
Challenges will come
Problems will be solved
Be patient as you grow
Share what you know
Dig a hole in the land…

ROOF TOP DREAMING

Roof top dreaming
Shining like a diamond
Straight succeeding
Always perfect timing
Roof top dreaming
Sunshine beaming
Smooth sailing
True chilling
Roof top dreaming
Writing and planning
Taking action
Pure satisfaction

SERGEANT PROMETHEUS

Sergeant Prometheus
Was marching down the street
PFC Caligullis
Was bopping to the beat
Sergeant Prometheus
Said "You think you on that block?"
"Straighten up and march
"Curl your fingers and don't talk
Left, Right, Left, Right, Left, Right, Hooah

SOLDIERS, GUNS AND BULLETS

Soldiers, Guns and Bullets Galore!
Soldiers, Guns and Bullets Galore!
Soldiers, Guns and Bullets Galore!
I make impossible possible
Conquer colossal obstacles
Any city we marching through
Turn your cities to Romper rooms
With our boots we'll be stomping you
Like a ghost we'll be haunting you
Even if you don't want us to
Soldiers, Guns and Bullets Galore!
Soldiers, Guns and Bullets Galore!
Soldiers, Guns and Bullets Galore!

SOME PEOPLE

Some people say "it ain't so"
Some people hate everywhere you go
Some of these people you won't even know
Still push it to the limit anyway
As I wait my turn patiently
It's none of my concern what you think of me
I'm still going to explode like dynamite
Take the road less traveled, let's dine tonight
Ask and you shall receive
Believe you deserve, what you need
Then take action
Your mind is a magnet
With a mental attraction
Do what needs to get done, right now
Some people say "it ain't so"

SUREFIRE YOUTH

Surefire Youth is the name
Character building is our thing
Respect one another all around
Building foundations from the ground
Surefire Youth is a household name
It's in our hearts
Pumping through our veins
See the STAAR in our eyes
Shining brightly from inside

SURVIVORS

Survive!!
Sur-viv-le!!
Survi-vors!!
Intestinal fortitude!
You have what it takes!
You have what you need!
Look, in the mirror…
Tell me what you see!
I see that soldier in you
You see that soldier in me
Let's get to going troop
Let's go all the way
Each and every day…
Survive!!
Sur-viv-le!!
Survivors!!!

SWEET SIXTEEN

16 months, 16 decisions
16 cuts, 16 incisions
M-16 so much precision
Load unload on 16 missions
Military life ain't easy believe me
You have to stand tall and fight for freedom
M-16, lock and load
40 out of 40 'til the block explode
Eagle eye I'm good to go
A soldier's life is the road I chose

THE MISSION

I coordinate the mission
I collaborate with fishes
The sharks and the whales
Game locked like a cell
Armed like an octopus
Vision like an eagle
All about the precious
Just like Smeagle
Lord of the ring
You can't afford to bang
I bring it full throttle
Kicking it like Tai-bo
You can't see me through an eye hole
I'm tougher then leather
Flyer then feathers
Heads get severed
On several occasions
I'm hotter then Cajon
I run with the made men
Bringing home the bacon
I coordinate the mission

TICK TOCK TICK

Tick tock tick
Time fly so quick
Like I have wings on my watch
On my watch on my wrist
Tock tick tock
Time doesn't stop
Like I have a green light
Green light on my watch
As time flies
I wonder where it goes
I ask myself this question
More then you'll ever know
I'm getting older and wiser
Molded by fire
Bolder then a tiger
Tick tock tick

TIME WAITS FOR NO MAN

Time waits for no man
The clock doesn't stop
Even if you cry tears
Till your eyeballs, Pop
I don't brag, I don't boast
I get bread, I make toast
Cadences ferocious
Your coma toast from the dosage
You have no choice but to cope with it
Time waits for no man
Maybe one more …. Tops!!
I say what I mean
I mean what I say

TRAIN IN THE RAIN

Train in the rain
Train on a train
Train on a deployment
How do you feel
This feeling is real
Man I go so hard
My whole body is steel
Train in the city
Train in front the TV
Train during an exercise
Training makes me want to pop lock
Let's train until our hearts stop
I'll savor every second
I'll enjoy every minute
Cherish every hour
My schedules never to hectic
Train in the rain

WALKED UP

I walked up to that DFAC(Dining Facility)
Washed my hands then sign my name
Got my fork, spoon and knife
I walked over to that salad bar
Got a lil lettuce, lil cheese, lil mater
Sat down, said grace then ate
Then I got a little thirsty
Man!!...I forgot my drink
Walked up to that "fridgerator"
Grabbed one water and one juice
Drunk them both down
Know tell me about you

WALK THE TALK

Don't just talk the talk
Walk the walk
Big dogs bark
Big dogs bite
Big dog float
Big dogs take flight
Talk it how you want to talk it
Walk it how you want to walk it
I'm not talking walkie talkies
When I say walking the talk

Don't just talk the talk
Walk the walk

WATCH

Watch what you think
Thoughts become words
Watch what you say
Words become action
Be careful what you do
Actions become character
Be careful what you wish for
You might just get it
I wish I was successful
I wish I was a millionaire

WHEN I PULL UP

When I pull up in that Rolls Royce Wraith
Please look us off up in our face
Tell us you believed from the start
This (US Army) is in our hearts
It pumps through our veins on the daily
I followed my dreams now they pay me
Military minded from the get go
Built my business on my block like Legos
I don't tangle with lame o's
money long, don't fold or jingle
When I pull up in that Rolls Royce Wraith

WIN OR LOSE

It's win or lose
Sin or snooze
Trim in the gym or
Binge on booze
Friend or foe
You choose
Permanent like tattoos
Classic like
Red and white 2's
Something like Jumpman
I get air time
Grizzly of a troop
And I use my mind

YOU GOTTA BELIEVE

You gotta believe
That you can succeed
And everything you need
You already got it
No sense in talking about it
Get on your grind and get it
Trouble gonna come
Just deal with it
I believe in me
I believe in you
I believe in we
I believe in us
To just believe is not enough
We must take action
You gotta believe

RUNNING CADENCE CANDY

ALL ARMY (NAVY, AIR FORCE, MARINES)

Two athletic soldiers were hooping in the gym
One said to the other, "I can look in the rim"
He said "I'm going to be an (All Army) hooper"
Jump hooks, step backs and alley-oopers
All Army hooper
Alley-oopers
Two athletic soldiers were swinging on a diamond
One said to the other "I'm grinding and shining"
He said "I'm going to be an (All Army) all-star
Live me a life traveling a far
(All Army) all-star
Two athletic soldiers and a boxing ring
One said to the other "I'm the boxing king"
He said "I'm over here Olympic dreaming"
Running ten miles in the morning and ten this evening
Olympic dreaming
Ten miles this evening

BATTLE BUDDY – (SHIPMATE, WINGMEN, DEVIL DOG)

Battle Buddy, Battle Buddy, has to have a battle buddy
PVT's has to have a Battle Buddy
SPC has to have a Battle Buddy
SGT has to have a Battle Buddy
Platoon SGT has to have a Battle Buddy
ISG has to have a Battle Buddy
SGM has to have a Battle Buddy
Battle Buddy x4

Butter bars has to have a Battle Buddy
ILT has to have a Battle Buddy
Captain has to have a Battle Buddy
Major has to have a Battle Buddy
LT-Col has to have a Battle Buddy
Col has to have a Battle Buddy
Generals has to have a Battle Buddy
Battle buddy x4
The President has to have a battle buddy…

BIG DOG (Jatavis Fuse)

(Caller) Give me that big dog
(Formation) Roof
Give me that big dog
Roof
Give me that German shepherd
Roof
Give me that mad dog
Roof
Give me that big dog
Roof
Give me that pit bull
Roof
Give me that bull dog
Roof
Give me that chi wha wha
Roof

BOB BAM

I knew this bear
His name was Bob Bam
He was a strong damn bear
Hell, he was a Bob Bam bear
He ran through the gate
He didn't want to be late
They asked for his I.D.
He said "Get Away from me!"
He ran down the street
He came to my house
He opened up my door
He was looking for some fear
He walked in my house
He was walking for some fear
He came in my room
He was searching for some fear
He tapped me on my shoulder
He was tapping for some fear
I opened up my eyes
I said "what you doing here?"
He looked me in my eyes
He said "I'm looking for some fear"
I laughed a little bit
He said "what you laughing for?"
So then I laughed a little bit more
He said "where is the fear?
I said "there ain't none in there!!
There ain't none in there (x2 or 3)
No fear
No fear
There ain't none in there!!

CHALLENGES

You got to plan your work
You got to work your plan
You'll be the man
By popular demand
In Iraq
Or Afghanistan
Can't you understand?
Challenges come and go
Tie your boots up
Come on let's go!
You got to plan your work
You got to work your plan

CONCRETE By: Jatavis Fuse

(Caller) Watch me make ya feet
(Formation) AYE!!
Beat up the concrete
AYE!!
Watch me make ya feet
AYE!!
Beat up the damn beat
AYE!!
Watch me make the beat
AYE!!
Turn up in the streets
AYE!!
Watch big SGT motivate cha
AYE!!

DO SOME PT

Do some PT (Physical Training)
Life got you down?
Do some PT
Section Sergeant on your back?
Do some PT
Platoon daddy got you down?
Do some PT
The Commander on your back?
Do some PT
LT got you down?
Do some PT
1SG on your back?
Do some PT

DONE, DONE (JATAVIS FUSE)

(Caller Transition) When that left foot strikes the
ground, all I want to hear is that "What" sound.
(Formation) What
They call me "Done, Done"
What
Done did it all
What
Run up and jump up the hill
What
They call me "Done, Done"
What
Done did it all
What
Deployment to Afghanistan
What

Don did it all
What
They call me "Done, Done"
What
Done did it all
What
Pump up and hype up the crowd
What
These streets
What
Done ran them all
What
They call me "Done, Done"

EVERYBODY SHINING

Everybody shining
My mind is the diamond type
They say that money talks
It's time to get your diamond right
We shining, we shining bla bla bling bling
Our minds and a diamond
Sa sa same thing!!

FANTASTIC

How do you feel?
I feel fantastic
Look at my feet
They feel fantastic
I feel my calves
They feel fantastic
I feel my knees
They feel fantastic
I feel my hips
They feel fantastic
My lower back
It feels fantastic
My upper back
It feels fantastic
My neck and skull
They feel fantastic

FULL BATTLE RATTLE

Full battle rattle
And a hundred degrees
Insurgents in the trees
Insurgents on their knees

Full battle rattle
And a hundred degrees
Stay hydrated
On the battle field please
Be a battle buddy for your battle and me

Full battle rattle
And a hundred degrees

GLADIATORS READY

Gladiators ready!!!
Spartans, where you at?
Warriors sound off!
Leaders, lead us!
We here now
Insurgents old news
Got my M -16
My combat boots
My camouflage
And my entrenching tool
Gladiators ready!!!
Spartans, where you at?
Warriors, sound off!
Leaders, lead us!
The U.S. needs us!

HATE FEEDS ME

Hate feeds me
I eat where the seeds meet
I'm ice cold
I bleed sleet
I can go acapella
I don't need beats
Just my heart thumping
And my blood pumping
This is the start of something
Bigger … then me
Figuratively
I dig in the beat
No shovel, no cleats
No pick, no rake
No ax, no mistakes
Capitol like the 50 States
I eat enemies
Till I empty the plate
Hate feed me!

HELL YEAH

"When that left, foot strikes the ground, all I want to
hear is that Hell Yeah"!!
Formation – Hell Yeah
Caller –Troops in the front
Formation – Hell Yeah
Caller -They must be Grunts
Formation – Hell Yeah
Caller -Troops in the middle
Formation – Hell Yeah
Caller -They wiggle wiggle
Formation – Hell Yeah
Caller -Troops in the back
Formation – Hell Yeah
Caller -Got rucks on their backs
Formation – Hell Yeah
Caller -They don't slack
Formation – Hell Yeah
Caller -Keeping soldiers in tact

HIGH AND TIGHT

Who got a high and tight?
SPC -------- got a high and tight!!
Who got that bald fade?
SGT -------- got that bald fade!!
Who got that clean shave?
LT --------- got that clean shave!!
Who got their eyebrows did?
CPT -------- eyebrows did!!

I AM

It's not by magic
You'll be physically fit
You have to look inside yourself
And work hard for it
It's not by osmosis
You'll be the truth
Believe in yourself
And your dreams will come trus
I am
We are
Soldiers
I am
A professional
I am
The best at what I do

ICE MAN

Ice man, ice man
Ice cold cadence
Ice man, ice man
Ice cold heart
Drinking ice cold drinks
The ice man wide wake
Ice man don't blink
Ice man, ice cold
The ice man never folds
Jack frost ain't the boss
The ice man got the sauce
Ice man, ice man

I CAN'T BE YOU

I can't be you
I'm too busy being me

I'm as busy as a bee
Steadily growing
Like a red wood tree

I can't be you
I'm too busy being me

I DON'T BEG

I don't beg
I don't borrow
No pain
No sorrow
In self pity
I don't wallow
I'm a leader
That can follow
I need me
To be me
I'm wide a wake
A real "G"

I DON'T DANCE

I don't dance anymore
I move to the rhythm
Like it's booze in my system
Drunk off ambition
Crunk like an engine
Forget about wishing
Dismiss schemes
And you can miss me
With thinking like a teen
I got a grown man swagger
To own land is the matter
Forget one fish, I want the whole platter
I don't dance anymore

IF YOU'RE SCARED

If you're scared, buy a dog
If you're scared, go to church
If you're scared, then why you joined
If you're scared go to church
If your scared buy a dog
See the Air Force, they protect the air
The Navy fights from sea to sea
Marines and Army, ground and pound
If you're scared, buy a dog
If you're scared, go to church
If you're scared, then why you joined

I'M A SHARK (IN THAT WATER)

I'm a shark in that water.
I'm a shark in that water!!
I'm a shark in that water!!!

I'm a statue in formation
I'm a monster in the field
I'm a soldier in this army
I'm a savage in the corps
I'm just like the God of war
I'm Kratos in the flesh
I'm a shark in that water

I'M NICE

I'm nice, I'm nice
I'm nicer than you'll ever be
I'm nice, I'm nice
Who do you know nicer than me
I'm nice, I'm nice
I'm nicer than you'll ever be
I'm nice, I'm nice
Who do you know nicer than me
I'm nice, I'm nice
I'm nicer than you'll ever be
I'm nice, I'm nice
Who do you know nicer than me

IN THE SKY

Look up in the sky
There's no limit
Look up in the sky
And see forever
Look up in the sky
The world is yours
Look up in the sky
The world is yours

I PARTY HARDY

I party hardy like a rock star
Farmer in the booth, I crop bars
Clean up man I could mop mars
1 everywhere I top charts
You can't run with me! I'll pop your heart
Master mind, I said master mind
I bring the rapture every time
Live after line, I shine by Design

I SAY WHAT I MEAN

I say what I mean
I mean what I say
I get respect without speaking
Like a green beret
Special forces
Celestial sources
Quality cadence
More zestful than yours is
I soak up knowledge like a sponge
Like a sponge in a puddle
Give you just enough wisdom

So, it's easy to funnel
You can tease me a bundle
But I'm beastly
So, suckas get pummeled
Or get molly whopped
Make them want to call the cops
Candy pants enemies
Sweeter then lollipops
Got your whole team saying
"Golly Gee Serge Stop"
We can't take much more
Maybe one more tops

I SHOT UP

I shot up in the ranks
Like a cook off in formation
US Army veteran
There is no debating
I practice "hurry up and wait"
Please don't try my patience

IT IS WHAT IT IS

Physical training
It is what it is
Push up and sit ups
It is what it is
5-mile run
It is what it is
12-month deployment
It is what it is
Accomplishing the mission
It is what it is
Studying for the board
It is what it is

IT'S YOUR MIND (Jatavis Fuse)

C.   It ain't your body
F.   What
C.   It's your mind!!
F.   What
C.   When your making love
F.   What
C.   To the double time
F.   What
C.   Said it ain't your body
F.   What
C.   It's your mind
F.   What
C.   When you're getting it in
F.   What
C.   To the double time
F.   What
C.   It ain't your body
F.   What
C.   It's your mind!!
F.   What
C.   It's your mind!!

KEEP GOING

Do what the clock does
Keep, keep going
You're in hot water
Keep, keep swimming
Push-ups need work
Keep, keep pushing
2-mile time too high
Keep, keep running
You want to rank up
Keep, keep studying
Keep, keep, keep going(High pitch voice)
Keep, keep, keep going
Keep, keep, keep going

LEAN (By: Eric White / Ronald Bartley)

I gotta pain
In my heart
And it's called
First Sergeant
Lean left
Lean right
Lean front
Lean back

I gotta pain
In my toe
And it's called
The C.O.
Lean left
Lean right
Lean front
Lean back

LET'S GO

(Unit name) Let's Gooooo!!
Throw on your PT shoes, and move toes!
Got to get to the finish line
I watch your back, you watch mine
Signal, Signal, Signal, Signal
(Unit name) Let's shoot
Get your full battle rattle, tie up your boots
Got to get to the finish line
I watch your back, and you watch mine
Signal, Signal, Signal, Signal

NEVER QUIT

A quitter never wins
A winner never quits
Don't stop get, get it
All is do is win
I never lose I only learn
Take away the "L"
All I do is earn
A quitter never wins
A winner never quits
Don't stop get, get it
Erase all doubt
Dictate the tempo
Time to get to work
Protect this house

NEXT STEP

When that left foot strikes the ground, all I want to
hear is "take the next step"
Take the next step
Sign up for basic training
Take the next step
Graduate basic training
Take the next step
Go to A.I.T.
Take the next step
Go to permanent party
Take the next step
Go to B L C
Take the next step
Graduate B L C
Take the next step
Go to A L C

Take the next step
Graduate A L C
Take the next step
Go to S L C
Take the next step
Graduate S L C
Take the next step
Go to 1SG course
Take the next step
Graduate 1SG course
Take the next step
Go to SGM course
Take the next step
Graduate…

NOTE: Formation says "Take the next step" on the left foot.

(P.T.) PHYSICAL TRAINING

P.T., P.T.
Push-ups and sit-ups
2-mile run
Cool down stretch
Now you're healthy
P.T., P.T.
I like it, I love it
I can't get enough of it
Oh, yeah
Oh, yeah
P.T., P.T.
Does a body right
Makes my cloths fit well
Now you're healthy
Now you're healthy

PIPE IT UP (By Jatavis Fuse)

C   Pipe it up, Pipe it up, Pipe it up, Pipe it up
F   Down, Down, Down
C   Alpha Company, we pipe it up!
F   Down
C   Bravo Company, we pipe it up!
F   Down
C   Pipe it up, Pipe it up, Pipe it up, Pipe it up

RUN UP

Run up in your area
Ain't nobody scared of you (ya)
Fight to the finish
I barley bark, the bites a bitch (bih)
Play with fire flip the switch
Make a hole, dig a ditch
I'm bringing rain, pitch a tent
You can't see me, limo tent
Run up in your area

RUNAWAY

You're a runaway car?
I'm a runaway truck!
You're a runaway truck?
I'm a runaway bus!
I'll run up and bust!
Put you in the dirt
Turn your bones into dust
Troop, you better pay homage
If you're fragile as eggs
Then I'll make omelets
Runaway when you see me in the distance
I'll spray on you busters in an instant
Misfits get hit quick, easy
Runaway, runaway, runaway

SHOT GUN!!

Shot Gun!! Shot Gun!!
Shot Gun!! Shot Gunn!!
Send me all the baddest
I'm a semi-automatic
See me in the attic
I'm addicted to the top
Shot Gun!! Shot Gun!!
Shot Gun!! Shot Gunn!!
So, toxic I'm a hazard in the booth
Shooting for the top!
Like the basket on the roof
Shot Gun, Shot Gun!!
Shot Gun Verbs
Each word straight shoot ya!

SOLDIER UP

Soldier up
On your feet
Soldier up
Get ready for war
Get your game face on
The day will be long
Get your gear up
Lace your boots up
Lock and load
Get ready
Don't get scared
It's gonna get heavy!

SPILT MILK

Spilt milk, spilt milk …
When I was an infant
I cried in an instant
When I became a toddler
I barley even bothered bra
As a pre-teen
I learned to be mean
In my teenage years
I barley shed tears
Now I'm almost thirty
I still represent the dirty
When I turn forty
I will assure thee
I won't cry over spilt milk
I'll spill forties
When I turn fifty
I'll still represent the filthy
Spilt milk, spilt milk

STRANGE TERRAIN

On strange terrain
I see the strangest thing
They tried to strangle the king
I got a known blood line
Unlike a strangers' veins
Forceful water flow
Like a fireman's hose
I'm on fire
Like a fireman's boots
And I'm fire proof
Like a fireman's shoes
Pants and jacket
I dance through your bracket
Fight stance automatic
Advanced fanatic
Causing havoc
On strange terrain

THEN I LEVELED UP

I studied for the board
Then I leveled up
I went to the board
Then I leveled up
I left, promotable
Then I leveled up
I went to WLC
Then I leveled up
I graduated WLC
Then I leveled up
I went to ALC
Then I leveled up
I went to SLC
Then I leveled up
I went to 1SG Course
Then I leveled up
I went to SGM Course
Then I leveled up
Army Green to Corporate Gray
Then I leveled up

THIS ARMY

This Army
Will make a man out of you!
This Army
Will make it do what it does!
This Army
Will make a man out of you!!
This Army
Is going to get your credit right!
This Army
Will have you fit to fight
This Army
Will help you reach your goals
This Army
Will help you push young Joes
This Army
Will help you see the world
This Army
Will get you a job referral

TIGER IN THE GAME

Tiger in the game
A real brave cat
Rolling with the waves
Like a wave cap
Leader of parades
Wave back
My cadences are legendary
So just step aside
When I'm stepping in the stair case
Or in the stair way
But don't stare please
Have you never seen a beast?
Tiger in the game!
A real brave cat!

TRIED AND TRUE

Beast mode, beast mode
I'm tried and true
I stick to the script
Don't apply the glue
I'm slick at the lip
You can't find a clue
Follow my lead
I won't hide the groove
Floating around this thing
It's like I glide to move
Toxic on the mic
Like fire booze
Sleep on me
Snooze and lose
Winner in the game
I choose to prove
Building from the basement
I move the tools
Even tempered
Rarely lose my cool
If I do get mad
I'm never mad at you
I'm mad at me
I'm that dude
My cadence sewn together
Like I used a spool
Check my thread count
I have yours times two
And if you're the MP's(Military Police)
I'm yelling "Hooty Who!!"

TRUTH BE TOLD

Truth be told
Facts
I love this life
Facts
Truth be told
Facts
I love loyalty
Facts
Truth be told
Facts
Determination
Facts
Truth be told
Facts
Respect the corps
Facts
Truth be told

WAH WAH WAH

Wah, Wah, Wah
Push ups, Sit ups
Get down get up
Burpees hurt me
SGT I'm thirsty
I want a slurpee
Wah Wah Wah
Push ups, Sit ups
Get down get up
Burpees hurt me
SGT I'm thirsty
I want a slurpee

WAKE UP

Wake up, wake up
Snooooze button
Get up, get up
Moooove something
Stretch out, stretch out
Who's coming
Early morning PT
Moooove something
Zero nine work call
Whoooo's coming
Wake up, wake up
Moooove something

WATER FLOW

Water flow
Super soaker
I ain't blowing smoke
I'll let the hooka choke ya
I get real crunk
I'm talking stupid stoked up
Wild Animal
Shark in a fish tank
Megalodon
I'm handling bombs
The man to your moms
Water flow

WE GOT ACTION

We got action
Iraq Deployment
We got action
Afghanistan
We got action
PT formation
We got action
Motor pool
We got action
Ed. center
We got action
Ruck March
We got action
Weapon range
We got action
Hey 1SG
We got action

Y'ALL TROOPS SOFT

Y'all troops soft like puddy and play doe
I'm surefire so I' flame on
Roll up to your spot, like my legs gone
Building foundations like Legos
Getting doe, cheddar cheese and Paso's
I got cadences by the case loads
No, eyes, nose or mouth, I still face foes
Send the bill, case closed
Flame starter
I bang harder
Smooth flow
Cool glow
Motivated
Dedicated
Fired up

YES, I'M IMPRESSED

Yes, I'm impressed
By your Teflon vest
I was a slept-on vet
Now I'm waking you up
Like coffee in your cup
Just dogging you pups
I got a lock on your guts
I got a Glock to your fronts
Holla back, holla back
Don't over-react
Classic Cadillac
Unseen cataract
With a wall to my back
I don't trust young slackers
Busters bass akwards (ass backwards)
Yes, I'm impressed

YOU CAN'T MURDER ME

You can't murder me
I'm like a herd of beast
Superhuman like Hercules
You are spicy you are crispy
You are chicken you are minced meat
And I'm a meat cleaver
Carnivore galore
Moving forward like a ford
Exploring all my options
Are we on the same accord?

YOU DON'T WANT TO BATTLE

You don't want to battle
I'll eat you like some cattle
Leave nothing but the bones
Now all the beef is gone
Troop you're chicken hearted
Your chick has departed
Now she's on my team
I bleed ambition
Bleed it out my veins
And it seeps
Through my seams
It's as simple as it seems
I cut through the chase
Like some Constantine
Constantine wire
I'm razor sharp
Blazing the top
And I'll never stop
You don't want to battle

AUTHOR BIOGRAPHIES

This index gives you information about each contributor and tells you where their contact information can be found.

Ronald Bartley raised in Norfolk, Virginia served 14 years on active duty. Bartley is currently an assistant coach for the All Army Basketball team. He also is a 5-time Gold medal winner with the All Armed Forces Basketball team. *www.coachup.com*

Jatavis Fuse king of the battle born and raised in Pahokee, Florida with over 12 years of active duty, as a Wheeled Vehicle Mechanic. He is an official member of the United States Allstar DJ's providing 15 years of professional Mobile Disc Jockey service around the world. Music is and always will be his passion. *djfuseusallstardjs@gmail.com*

Brett Thomas raised in Hardeeville, South Carolina, served 13 years on active duty as a Cable Systems Installer Maintainer. He is the author of *Velvet Actions and Velvet Activities the series.* Thomas is the owner and operator of *See Beyond Yourself Productions LLC DBA Surefire Youth* ™. *www.surefireyouth.com*

Kareena Thomas is co-founder of *See Beyond Yourself Productions LLC DBA Surefire Youth*™. Kareena has had an illustrious career as a Child Care professional and world renowned chief. *www.surefireyouth.com*

Made in the USA
Charleston, SC
02 February 2017